A Note to Parents

DK READERS is a compelling program for beginning readers, designed in conjunction with leading literacy experts, including Dr. Linda Gambrell, Professor of Education at Clemson University. Dr. Gambrell has served as President of the International Reading Association, National Reading Conference, and College Reading Association.

Beautiful illustrations and superb full-color photographs combine with engaging, easy-to-read stories and informational texts to offer a fresh approach to each subject in the series. Each DK READER is guaranteed to capture a child's interest while developing his or her reading skills, general knowledge, and love of reading.

The five levels of DK READERS are aimed at different reading abilities, enabling you to choose the books that are exactly right for your child:

> **Pre-level 1**: Learning to read
>
> **Level 1**: Beginning to read
>
> **Level 2**: Beginning to read alone
>
> **Level 3**: Reading alone
>
> **Level 4**: Proficient readers

The "normal" age at which a child begins to read can be anywhere from three to eight years old. Adult participation through the lower levels is very helpful for providing encouragement, discussing storylines, and sounding out unfamiliar words.

No matter which level you select, you can be sure that you are helping your child learn to read, then read to learn!

LONDON, NEW YORK,
MELBOURNE, MUNICH, AND DELHI

Editor Victoria Taylor
Designer Jon Hall
Senior Designer Lynne Moulding
Brand Manager Ron Stobbart
Art Director Lisa Lanzarini
Managing Editor Catherine Saunders
Publishing Manager Simon Beecroft
Category Publisher Alex Allan
Production Controller Clare McLean
Production Editor Siu Chan

Reading Consultant
Linda B. Gambrell, Ph.D.

First published in the United States in 2009
by DK Publishing
375 Hudson Street
New York, New York 10014

11 12 13 10 9 8 7 6 5 4
005–DD527—01/09

DK Books are available at special discounts when purchased in bulk
for sales promotions, premiums, fund-raising, or educational use.
For details, contact: DK Publishing Special Markets,
375 Hudson Street, New York, New York 10014
SpecialSales@dk.com

Published in Great Britain by Dorling Kindersley Limited.
A catalog record for this book is available from the Library of Congress.

ISBN: 978-0-7566-4521-2 (Paperback)
ISBN: 978-0-7566-4520-5 (Hardback)

Color reproduction by MDP
Printed and bound in the U.S.A. by Lake Book Manufacturing, Inc.

Discover more at
www.dk.com
www.LEGO.com

DK READERS

BEGINNING 1 TO READ

Around Town

Written by Victoria Taylor

It's the start of another busy day in LEGO® Ville!

Early in the morning the road
sweeper makes the town clean.

A delivery for the supermarket arrives at the railway station.

The supermarket opens
and people begin to go in
to buy bread for breakfast.

What's this?

There is a fire!

The fire truck rushes to the fire with its siren blaring.

One of the firemen
tries very hard to
put out the flames.
A difficult job!

The flames are very big now.
The firefighter is having trouble
battling the flames on his own.

Help arrives. It's a helicopter!

The helicopter uses a hose to spray water on the flames. It works!

The firefighters have done a good job. Everything is safe now.

Back in town the builders are
hard at work on the building site.

They are building a new house.

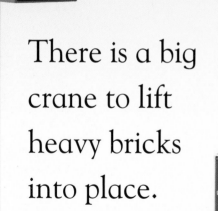

There is a big
crane to lift
heavy bricks
into place.

The builders always wear their hard hats while they work.

A cement mixer is making cement.

Cement is used to stick bricks
together for building walls.

The LEGO Ville mechanics are fixing people's cars.

This car has broken down, but the mechanics know what to do.

There are lots of
visitors at the zoo
on this sunny day.

ZOO

ZOO

The monkeys are showing off to the visitors by swinging around!

It's lunchtime for the animals.

The zoo keepers take the right
food to each animal.

The LEGO Ville police hear that someone has stolen a cake from the supermarket!

The police rush in to the
supermarket to see if they
can catch the thief.

The police dog catches the thief.
He could smell the cake!

It has been another successful day in LEGO Ville.

Quiz!

1. What helped the firetruck put out the fire?

2. What were the builders making?

3. What is this man's job?

4. What did the thief steal?

Answers: 1. a helicopter/hose 2. a house 3. a mechanic 4. a cake